SLIDE & SLACK KEY

Ukulele

BY *Fred Sokolow*

EDITED BY RONNY S. SCHIFF

RECORDING:
Guitar and vocals: Fred Sokolow
Sound Engineer: Michael Monagan
Recorded and Mixed at Sossity Sound

PLAYBACK+
Speed · Pitch · Balance · Loop

To access audio visit:
www.halleonard.com/mylibrary

Enter Code
4892-3838-3990-2578

ISBN 978-1-4950-3613-2

HAL•LEONARD®
CORPORATION
7777 W. BLUEMOUND RD. P.O. BOX 13819 MILWAUKEE, WI 53213

In Australia Contact:
Hal Leonard Australia Pty. Ltd.
4 Lentara Court
Cheltenham, Victoria, 3192 Australia
Email: ausadmin@halleonard.com.au

Visit Hal Leonard Online at
www.halleonard.com

INTRODUCTION

Bottleneck or slide playing is soulful and evocative, whether it's employed in blues, gospel, country, or rock music. Hawaiian slack key playing is known for its mellow, magical, even mystical vibe. Both techniques are associated with guitar played in open tunings, but there are plenty of reasons to play these musical styles on the ukulele. For one thing, they are both part of Hawaiian tradition.

Though the uke evolved from a Portuguese instrument, its worldwide popularity emanated from Hawai'i and Hawaiian music. Slack key guitar, in which the guitar is fingerpicked in an open tuning, is uniquely Hawaiian as well. Its roots date back to the early 1800s when European "cowboys" brought guitars to the islands, and Hawaiians created their own style of guitar music. So it's only logical to try slack key on the ukulele and blend two closely related traditions.

As for slide playing, many historians believe that lap-style, steel guitar playing began in Hawai'i. One legend has it that Joseph Kekuko, walking along a railroad track in the late 1800s, picked up a metal bolt and slid it on his guitar strings with an enchanting effect. Another apocryphal story claims that a Hawaiian guitarist's comb fell out of his hair and landed on his guitar, creating an intriguing, sliding sound. One or both of these experiments led to the creation of the lap steel, also known as a Hawaiian guitar. This instrument became a trademark of Hawaiian music and, in the 1920s, crossed over to mainland country music as well. At the same time, African Americans were using pieces of pipe, jacknives, and bottlenecks to slide on guitar strings and play the blues while holding the instrument upright. This allows one to slide and, if desired, play chords as well (something that's hard to do while playing lap style).

Since slide playing is so much a part of Hawaiian music, why not extend it to the uke? And, while you're at it, why not use a slide to play blues or "sacred steel" (gospel music played on a lap or pedal steel) on the uke, as well?

Of course, there's another reason to play slide and slack key on the ukulele: Now that the uke is conceivably even more popular than it was in the 1920s, ukists are playing everything from classical music to heavy metal on the instrument. So, this collection of tunes, licks, and techniques is just part of the inevitable movement to expand the uke's (and your) musical horizons. Anything is possible on this small but mighty instrument!

This book teaches how to play slide in two open tunings (open C and open G), as well as standard tuning. It also shows how to fingerpick—slack key style—in the same two open tunings, moving chords up and down the fretboard to achieve that beautiful, relaxed, slack-key sound. In addition to learning several great tunes, you'll come away with some jamming techniques and some licks and ideas you can apply to many other musical genres. Enjoy the tunes and instruction in this offering!

Fred Sokolow

Contents

PRELIMINARIES

CHOOSING A SLIDE

Your local or online music store has glass, metal, ceramic, and plastic slides, as well as thick- and thin-walled slides. These choices are all about your personal taste. However, there are some practical differences:

- Real bottlenecks often have a curvature. If that curvature doesn't match your flat fretboard, use a straight, cylindrical slide.

- Your slide should be long enough to span all four strings.

- Get one that fits your finger snugly, but not too tightly. And this opens up another can of worms: which finger?

HOW TO USE THE SLIDE

Opinions on this subject abound. Some put the slide on the ring finger, the index finger, or the middle finger (Bonnie Raitt does the latter). Most prefer to wear the slide on the little finger, because it leaves the rest of your hand free to play chords and to mute the strings behind the slide. Here are some other pointers with regards to handling the slide:

- Go lightly. If you press down too hard on the strings, you'll hear the slide drag over the frets.

- With the slide on your little finger, you can dampen the strings with your ring finger, behind the slide, to cut down on unwanted noises.

- *Vibrato* is an important part of slide playing. It's that wobble you get by shaking the slide on a sustained note in order to imitate the vibrato of a singing voice. It's all in the left hand. To get vibrato on a string, anchor your left-hand thumb against the back of the neck and shake your hand from the wrist. Here's how it looks in music/tablature:

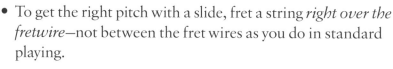

- To get the right pitch with a slide, fret a string *right over the fretwire*—not between the fret wires as you do in standard playing.

- Intonation (getting the right pitch) is all-important. Theoretically, it's easy. All you have to do is listen. While aiming for the right note, if you overshoot or undershoot, adjust the slide up or down with a little vibrato.

Slide can also be played lap style on the uke, though you can't play chords while holding the uke in this position:

C Tuning

It's possible to play slide in standard tuning, but old-school slide players usually tune to an open chord. This is partly because you get a nice droning effect when your instrument is tuned that way, but it's also easier than playing in standard tuning.

The good news about C tuning is that you only have to retune one string. The first string (A) is tuned down to G. Do this, strum across the open (unfretted) strings, and you'll hear a C major chord.

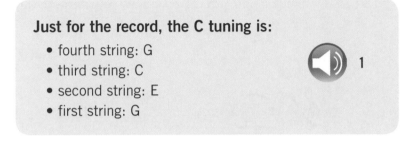

Just for the record, the C tuning is:
- fourth string: G
- third string: C
- second string: E
- first string: G

1

A lot of playing in this tuning involves barring across all four strings with the slide, playing major chords like these:

D

F

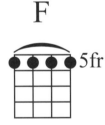
5fr

G

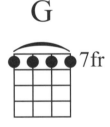
7fr

SLIDE IN C TUNING

The C tuning resembles the Mississippi Delta G tuning used by many blues guitarists, so you'll start with "Betty and Dupree," an old 12-bar blues tune. To get you used to using a slide, here's a simple strumming backup to it. The F chord is a barre across the 5th fret, and the G is at the 7th fret. In this accompaniment, you slide up to each chord from one or two frets back. There are a few very simple *fills*—melodic phrases that fill the gaps in the vocal line.

Be aware of these tab/music notations:

- A line connecting one note to another (in tab and music notation) indicates a slide. If there's a slur (curved line) above the slide, only the first note is to be picked. If there is no slur, you pick the first note, slide up to the second, and pick it as well.

- A line on the left side of a musical note or tab number means you slide up to the given note from one or two frets back—i.e., you pick a note a few frets below your target note and slide up into it.

C Tuning

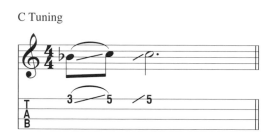

Betty and Dupree
Backup

2

In the following solo for "Betty and Dupree," many of the melody notes are in the barred chords. The fills are a little more elaborate. There's also some vibrato (described in the "Preliminaries" chapter).

To play a single note on the first string that's not part of a chord (as in bar 11 of the following solo), lower and/or angle your slide so that it touches the first string and not the other strings. To play single notes on other strings (like the very first notes), try to angle the slide so it only touches the indicated string.

Just the first string

Just the third string

Betty and Dupree
Solo

Notice the C7 chord in the fourth bar of "Betty and Dupree." Here's a full C7 chord:

C7

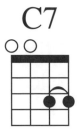

As you learn more solos, you'll notice that some melody notes come from the barred chords (F and G in "Betty and Dupree"), and others are found within the first few frets. To speed up your ability to find melody notes in the first five frets of the uke, practice playing this C major scale:

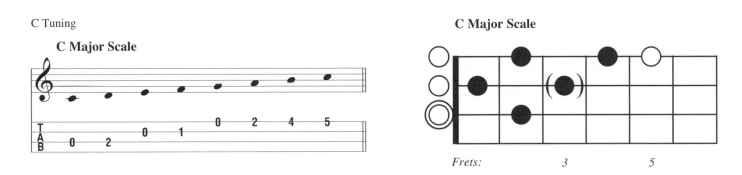

Blues tunes may also include "blue notes" that are not in the major scale:

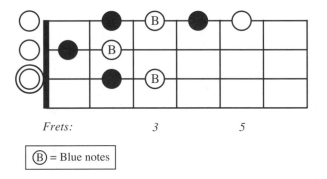

Ⓑ = Blue notes

"John Henry" is an old folk tune that's been played by blues, country, bluegrass, and old-time musicians for nearly a century. As in "Betty and Dupree," some of the melody notes come from the barred chords, and some come from the C major scale in the first few frets.

John Henry
Solo

To play the opening notes of "John Henry," and in several other places in the solo, you have to tip the slide, or bring it down to the first string, as described previously before the "Betty and Dupree" solo.

"Uke-ing the Blues" is another 12-bar tune that employs some typical blues moves, such as the "passing" F and E♭ chords in the first three bars, which create a bluesy riff. Also notice the F7 in bar 6: just as you fretted the first and second strings three frets above the open C to play a C7, you can play an F7 by fretting those same strings three frets above the barred F chord. In fact, you can play any 7th chord by playing the first and second strings three frets above a barred chord:

Uke-ing the Blues

5

"Wreck of Old 97" is a popular country and bluegrass standard that describes an actual train wreck that occurred in Virginia in 1902. The following solo shows how slide uke can sound country as well as bluesy.

Wreck of Old 97

6

C Tuning

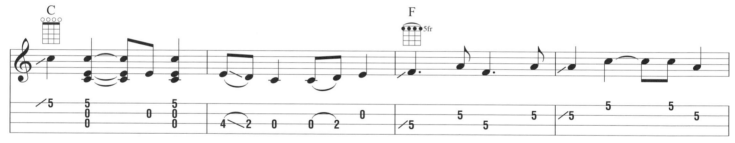

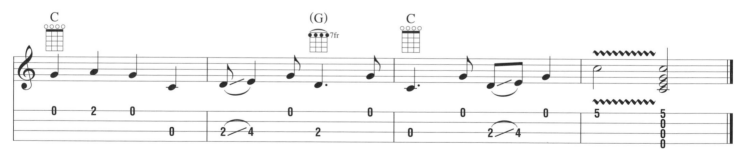

Just because you're in C tuning doesn't mean you have to play in the key of C! Some tunes are very playable in other keys, like this key-of-F version of the old folk tune, "I Never Will Marry." Notice the B♭ chord:

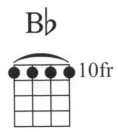

I Never Will Marry
Key of F

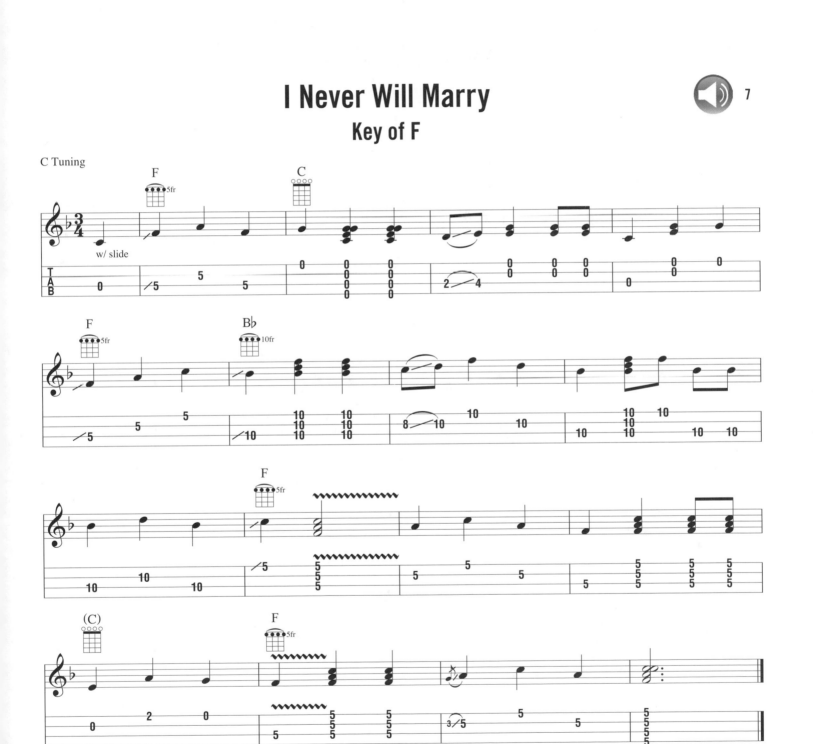

It's not difficult to move "I Never Will Marry" up two frets and play it in the key of G. Try it! It includes a barred D chord:

I Never Will Marry
Key of G

Here's the classic gospel tune, "When the Saints Go Marching In," in the key of G.

When the Saints Go Marching In
Key of G

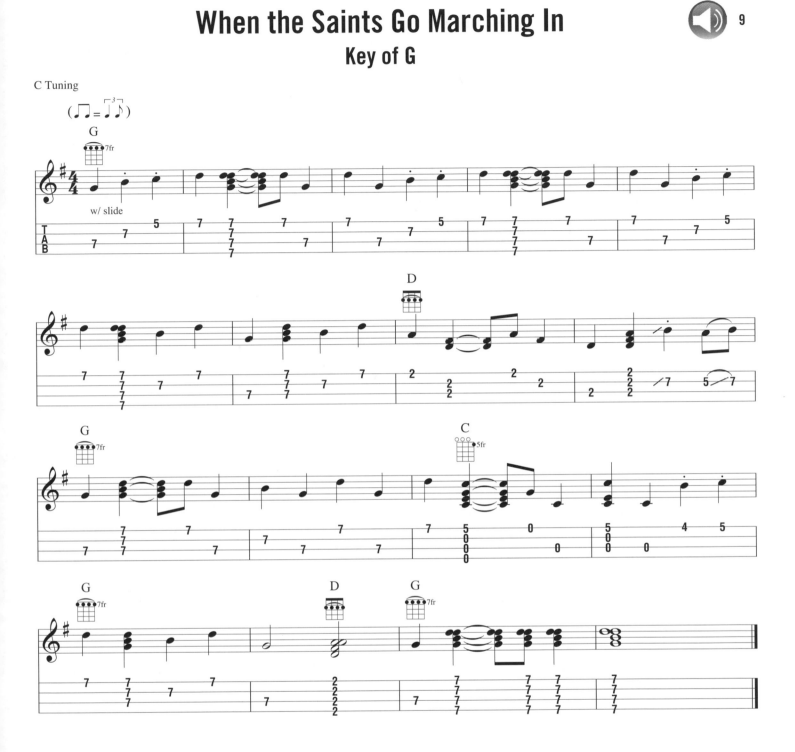

IMPROVISING IN C TUNING

Whether you're playing solo or with other players, you can improvise with a slide in C tuning. Here are a few tips on how to make up licks that fit a song:

- To ad lib on the open C chord, build licks (musical phrases) out of the C major scale and include occasional blue notes, like this:

- Go with the chord changes! Slide up to the appropriate chord and make up licks by playing the notes in that barred chord. For example, if the given chord is F, you can play licks like this:

- Make up more licks by combining the barred chord's notes with notes that are one or two frets behind the barre, like this:

12

There are two important points to notice about these licks:
1. They almost always end at the barred chord.
2. You often play a lower note by moving back to the barred chord *on a lower string*, as seen at the end of licks A and E (above) as well as the beginning of lick B.

- The first and second strings, played three frets above a barre, create a 7th chord. You can build additional licks using that idea. For example:

13

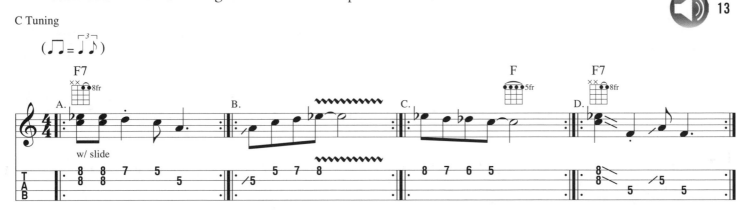

These improvising ideas apply to any type of music—blues, rock, country, whatever! To illustrate how it's done, here's an ad-lib solo for a basic rock progression.

Standard Rock Progression in C

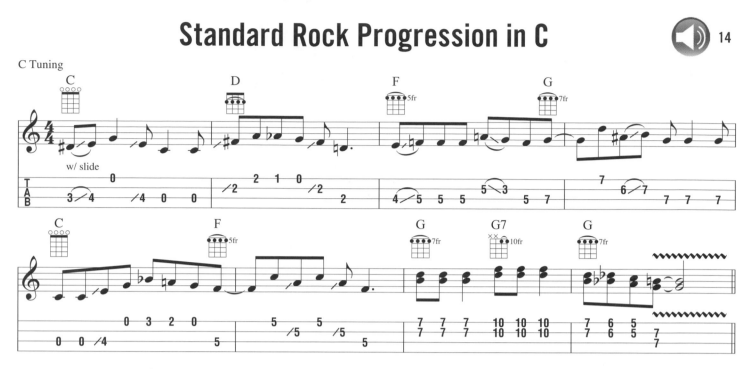

AD-LIBBING SLIDE IN OTHER KEYS

The arrangements of "I Never Will Marry" in this chapter illustrate that you can play slide in any key while tuned to C tuning. The same principles apply: follow a song's chord changes with barred chords, make up licks at the barre and one or two frets behind the barre, and so on. For example, here's "Standard Rock Progression" in the key of G:

Standard Rock Progression in G

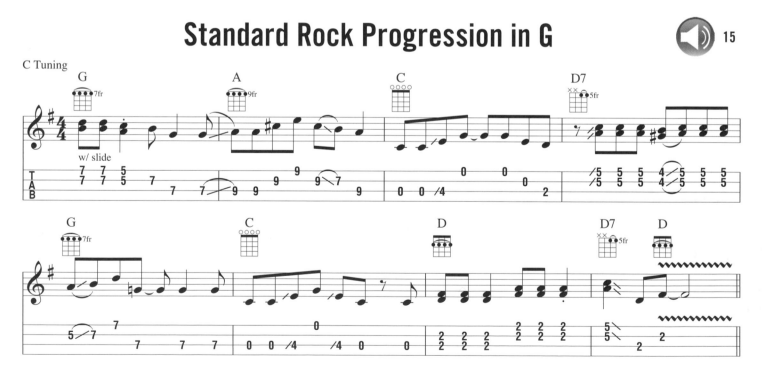

Play along with the tracks that go with this chapter and instead of duplicating the written-out solos, use the above improvising strategies to make up your own. Then try ad-libbing solos with other players. It's one of the best ways to have fun with slide uke!

SLACK KEY IN C TUNING

Slack key artists call the Delta blues/open G tuning (D–G–D–G–B–D on guitar) the "taro patch" tuning. As already mentioned, this resembles the uke's open C tuning (G–C–E–G). So, if you just worked your way through the previous chapter ("Slide in C Tuning"), keep your uke tuned to open C and learn some "taro patch" slack key tunes.

FINGERPICKING AND ROLLS

The right-hand technique in slack key playing differs from the strumming-and-picking-out-occasional-melody-notes method you learned in the slide tunes. Slack key players fingerpick a steady, rolling rhythm that never lets up and creates an almost hypnotic effect. On guitar, this often involves the alternating thumb-bass picking associated with Merle Travis and blues players like Mississippi John Hurt or Blind Blake. On a uke with a high G, the fingerpicking patterns keep changing, but the result is the same: the song's melody is surrounded by grace notes or "filler notes"—i.e., extra notes that surround the melody and keep the rhythm going.

The following three-finger patterns, similar to Scruggs-style banjo rolls, create the steady, rolling rhythm that's characteristic of slack key style. To help develop your right-hand picking, practice the following one-bar rolls over and over until they flow smoothly:

🔊 16

Note: Pay attention to the right-hand fingerings shown: p = thumb, i = index, and m = middle.

CHORDS

Most of the chords you learned in the previous chapter are played by barring all or some of the strings with the slide. To play slack key style, you need actual chords! To get you started, familiarize yourself with the following chord shapes. They're identical to the chords you already play on a normally tuned uke (G–C–E–A), except for the first string. Since the first string is tuned down two frets lower than usual, all the standard chords include a "two-frets-higher-than-usual" first string.

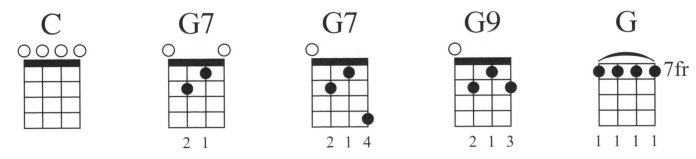

Your first slack key tune is "Manu Kapalulu," written in the late 1800s by Queen Lili'uokalani, the last Hawaiian queen. A prolific songwriter, she wrote the famous "Aloha Oe" and many other tunes that have become standards—still sung, danced to, and played by slack key artists wherever Hawaiian music is performed. Quite a few of her compositions are included in this book. "Manu Kapalulu" is literally about a quail, but it's really about someone with whom the queen was annoyed!

In this tune, and all the slack key songs that follow, emphasize the melody notes by playing them louder than the filler notes, so that each song's unique melody stands out. Listening to the music tracks will help you do this. Also, notice that the arrangement is not non-stop fingerpicking; there are occasional strums to express the tune's chord changes. Strum up with your index finger or down with your thumb. The tempo is "cut time," with a sort of a country feel.

Manu Kapalulu

The next tune, "Ninipo," is over a hundred years old. There's a YouTube video of the song played as a fast march that is taken from a 1909 Edison cylinder! The song concerns the Hawaiian goddess Pele's jealousy of the relationship between her sister Hiʻiaka and Hiʻaka's friend Hopoe.

The arrangement below is in cut time but much slower than the 1909 version. It includes a few new chord shapes:

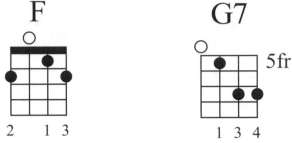

Ninipo

18

"Sanoe," which means "drifting over the mountains," is another Queen Liliʻuokalani composition. The song concerns a secret court love affair. It was originally written in 4/4 time, but most people play it in 6/8 time. It features two new chords:

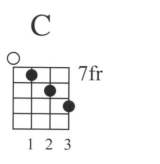

Sanoe

C Tuning

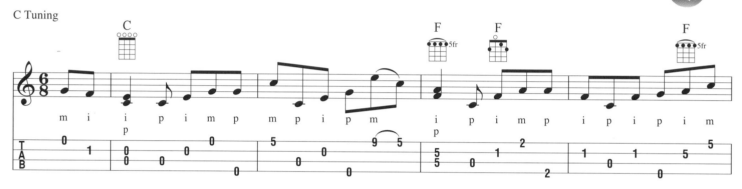

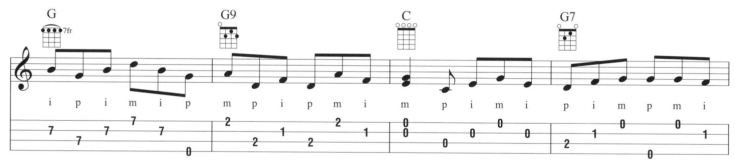

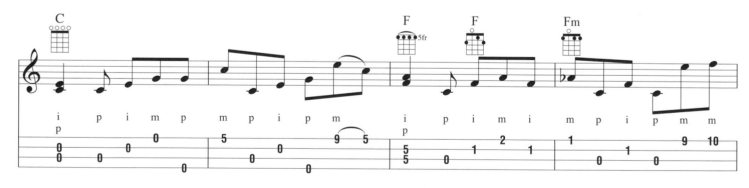

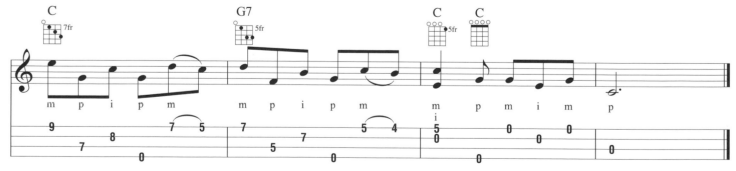

Written by Charles E. King in 1916, "Imi Au La Oe"—also called "The King's Serenade"—translates as "I am searching for you." It was featured in the operetta *Prince of Hawaii*, on which two Hollywood films were loosely based, both called *Bird of Paradise* (1932 and 1951).

The arrangement that follows goes twice around the 16-bar tune. The second version is an octave higher than the first. Both versions feature pairs of notes, because the melody is harmonized with notes that are a 3rd higher. The harmonies create a very pretty effect. There are two new chord shapes in the higher section:

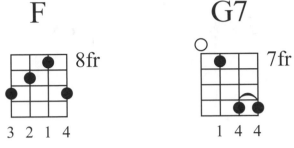

Continue using the same method of pluck-hand fingering as notated in the previous songs.

Imi Au La Oe

20

Yet another waltz, "Ahe Lau Makani" was written in 1868 by Queen Liliʻuokalani with her sister Likelike and an un-named collaborator. The title means "the soft gentle breeze," but the breeze in this love song is the breath of a lover. The second section of the tune begins like the first section but goes in a different direction melodically, taking you up the fretboard to include several up-the-neck chords you've already played:

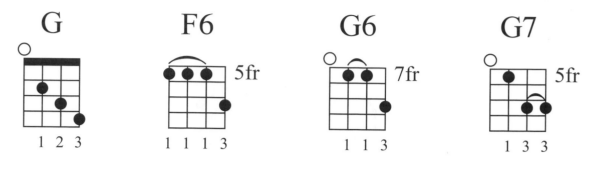

Ahe Lau Makani

21

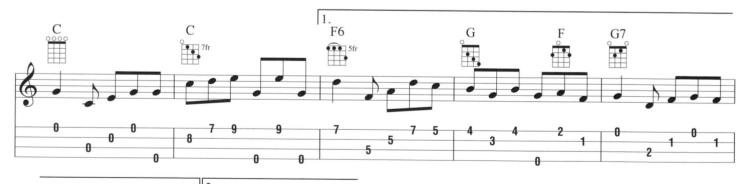

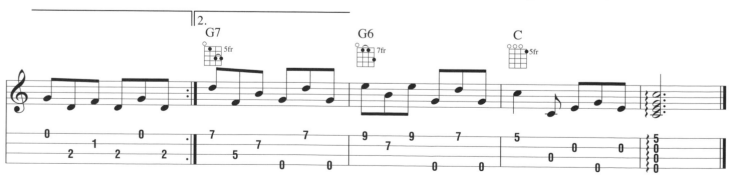

Written in 1860, "Nani Na Pua Ko'olau" is probably Queen Lili'uokalani's first published work. The title means "flower of Ko'olau," and, as in many Hawaiian tunes, the lyrics mix romantic images with references to the beauties of nature. The following arrangement is played in straight-eighths fashion. It has two sections and includes these up-the-neck chords:

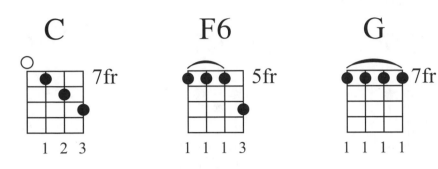

Nani Na Pua Ko'olau

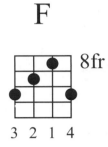
22

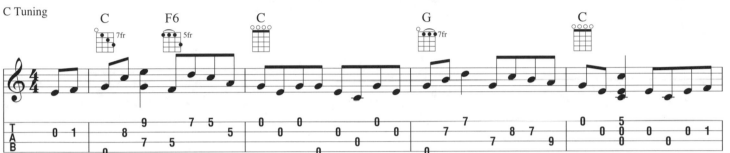

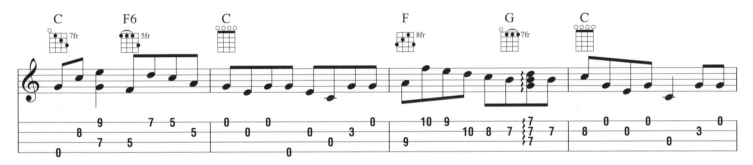

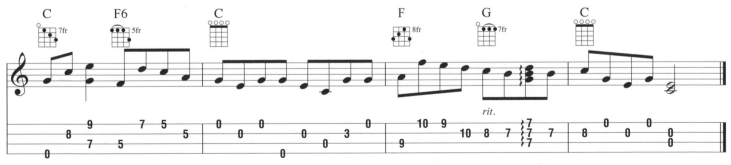

Queen Liliʻuokalani wrote "Kuʻu Pua I Paoakalani" when she was imprisoned by U.S. forces that took over Hawaiʻi in a military coup. The song's title means "my flowers at Paoakalani," and it's a tribute to a loyal friend who brought her flowers wrapped in newspaper daily. Since the queen was forbidden any news of the outside world, the daily delivery was a ruse that circumvented this ban. This arrangement of this beautiful, two-part tune includes these up-the-neck chords:

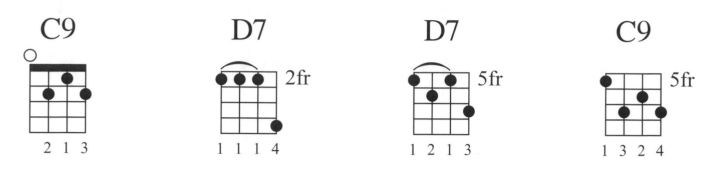

Kuʻu Pua I Paoakalani

23

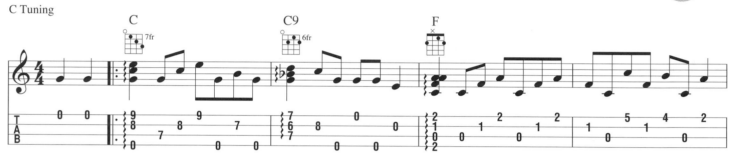

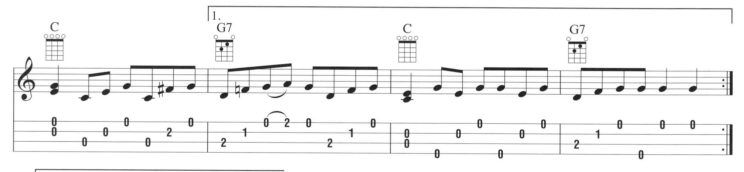

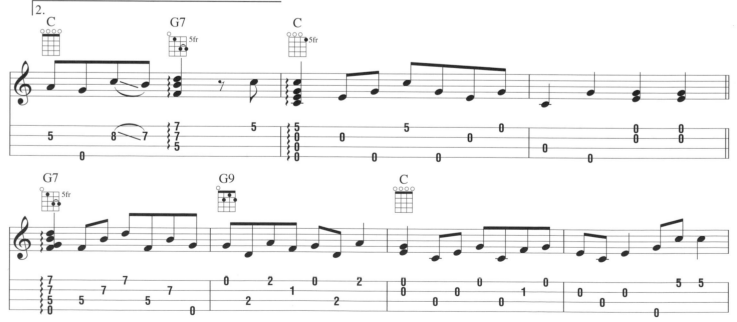

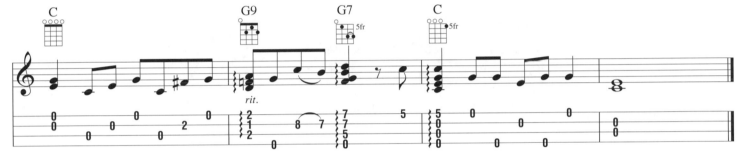

MAKING UP YOUR OWN ARRANGEMENTS

Besides memorizing the slack key arrangements in this book, try noodling around on the uke in open C tuning using the chords you've learned so far. And feel free to invent your own chords! Eventually, you may want to make up your own arrangements of tunes. If that's a goal, familiarity with the C major scale will be helpful to you. When putting together an arrangement of a song, here's the process to follow:

1. Strum the chords in a steady rhythm and hum the tune.

2. Pick out the melody to the tune, also in a steady rhythm, with the same pauses that occur when you sing/hum the melody. Fret the appropriate chord shapes while you're doing this.

3. Repeat Step 2, but this time fill out the melody by playing rolls during pauses or sustained melody notes. When the melody consists of quarter notes, add grace notes or "filler notes" (from the appropriate chord) between some of the melody notes.

There are an infinite number of ways to fill out the melody with rolls, so do whatever comes naturally to your picking hand (assuming you've practiced the rolls at the beginning of this chapter). Also, feel free to vary the melody somewhat. If you listen to several slack key players' versions of a particular song, you'll hear how much variation is accepted in this style of music!

G Tuning

Among slide and open-tuning guitarists, D tuning is just as popular as open G. Blues, rock, and country guitarists often use open D—some exclusively, others on occasion. Some examples include Blind Willie Johnson, Doc Watson, Elmore James, Dave Lindley, and Maybelle Carter (on a few tunes). Duane Allman usually played in open E, which is the same as open D, only tuned up a whole step (two frets) higher. Bob Dylan played about half of his famous "Blood on the Tracks" album in open E.

On the ukulele, open D translates easily to open G. If you tune a guitar to open D and capo up five frets, the four treble strings sound like a uke tuned to open G with no capo (except the fourth string is an octave higher than on a guitar). To get to open G, you have to lower three strings. Starting with the fourth/G string, it's G–B–D–G. Only the fourth string G remains the same as in standard tuning:

G tuning is:
- The fourth string remains the same.
- Tune the third string (C) down to B.
- Tune the second string (E) down to D.
- Tune the first string (A) down to G.

🔊 24

Once you've tuned down to the open G chord, try these new barred chords:

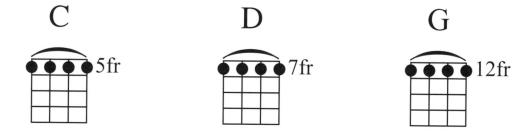

SLIDE IN G TUNING

Here's a 12-bar blues solo in G that'll get you started sliding in G tuning. Sometimes, you'll be strumming barred chords, two or three strings at a time. Other times, you'll be playing bluesy single-note licks. These licks are made up of notes in the barred chord or one or two frets below the barred chord (see the chapter on "Slide in C Tuning"). You can make up any number of licks using these few notes and keep coming back to the barred chord for resolution.

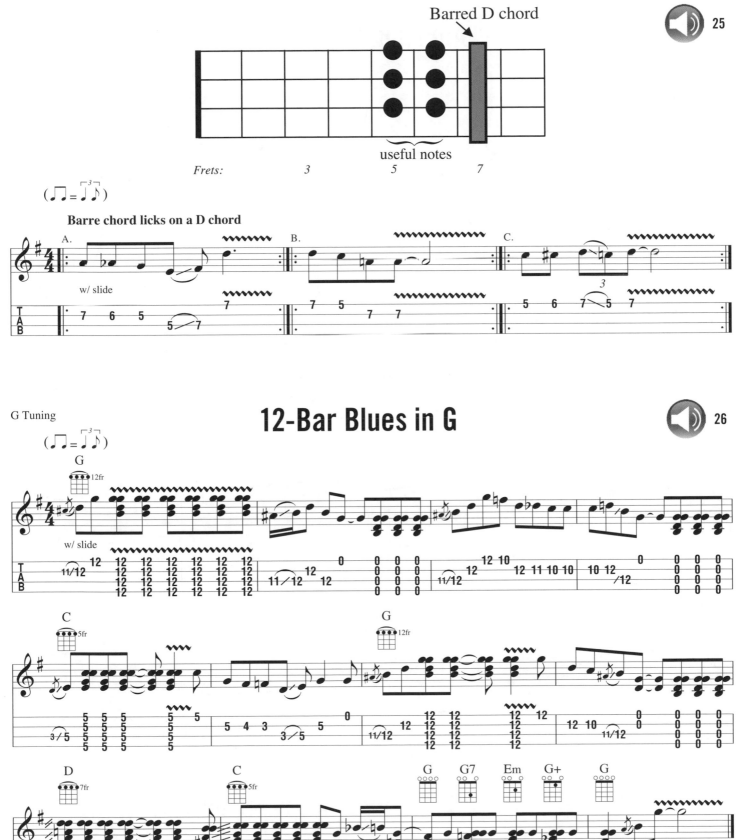

The last two bars of "12-Bar Blues in G" are a *turnaround*: a common lick in blues tunes that signals the end of a 12- or 8-bar sequence. Typically, this turnaround features a descending melodic line.

Here's a slide-type arrangement of the gospel classic "Amazing Grace" in open G. It begins with a slide up to the second string/5th fret. This is the same note as the open first string (G), but playing it on the second string/5th fret has more character, because you can add vibrato and sustain that fretted G note.

Amazing Grace

If you're familiar with the first-position G major scale, it's easier to pick out melodies in G. Here it is:

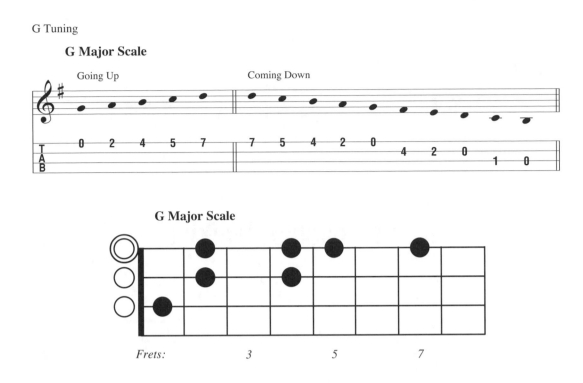

"Aloha Oe (Farewell to Thee)" was composed by the Hawaiian queen Lili'uokalani circa 1877. It's one of Hawai'i's most famous songs. In the following arrangement (as in the last two songs), many of the melody notes are found within barred chords. Other notes are one or two frets below the barre.

Aloha Oe

28

The G chord at the 12th fret is played with *harmonics*. Instead of barring at the 12th fret, touch the strings lightly with your barring finger, right over the fretwire (instead of between the fretwires), strum the chord, and immediately pull the barring finger away from the strings to let them ring out, as heard on the track.

"On the Beach at Waikiki" is a popular *hapa haole* song (part in English, part in Hawaiian) from 1916. It includes barred E♭, A, and F♯ chords:

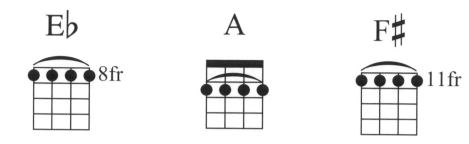

On the Beach at Waikiki

29

"Beautiful Brown Eyes," a traditional folk tune popularized by many country artists, includes a D7 chord. To play any 7th chord, fret the second and third strings three frets above a barred chord:

Beautiful Brown Eyes

The gospel standard "Oh Mary, Don't You Weep" works well in G tuning.

Oh Mary, Don't You Weep

G Tuning

"This Little Light of Mine" is another gospel standard that is also popular among folk artists. The solo includes two new chords: a barred B and an Em, the latter of which is played with the fingers instead of the slide. (You saw the Em chord briefly during the turnaround lick in "12-Bar Blues in G.")

This Little Light of Mine

"Keep Your Lamp Trimmed and Burning" is yet another gospel tune that has been performed and recorded by many blues and gospel artists for about a century. This version is a cross between Blind Willie Johnson's and Skip James's interpretations.

Keep Your Lamp Trimmed and Burning

SLACK KEY IN G TUNING

"Open G" tuning is just as useful for slack key style as it is for slide. Some tunes are impossible to play in open C, because the melody takes you all the way up to the 12th–15th frets (or higher), where the uke starts to sound as though it's being played by chipmunks. Those same tunes may sit easily on the first seven frets in G tuning!

CHORDS

A new set of chords is called for. Many of them resemble C tuning chords "moved up a string," like this:

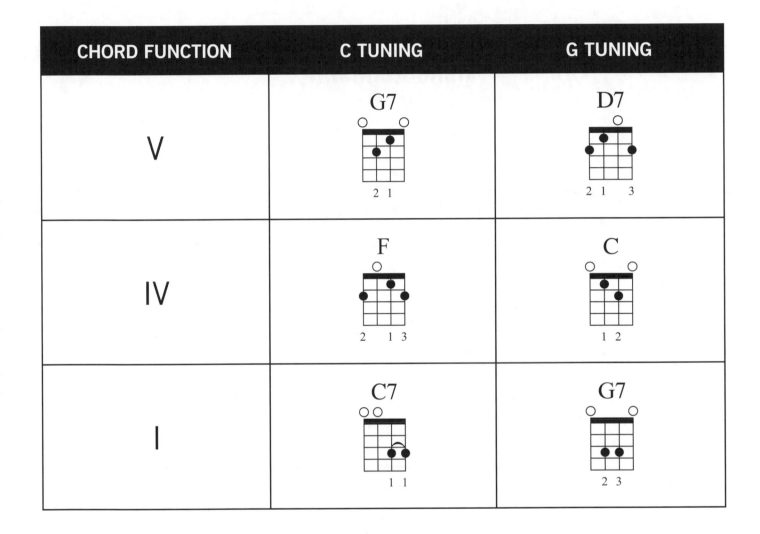

CHORD FUNCTION	C TUNING	G TUNING
V	G7	D7
IV	F	C
I	C7	G7

Note: Since the first and fourth strings are both tuned to G, they are often fretted at the same fret.

Your first open G tune is "Manu Kapalulu." Like many of the tunes in this chapter, you will be familiar with the melody to this song, because you played it in the "Slack Key in C Tuning" chapter. Many of the melody notes are the same as in the open C arrangement, only "moved up a string."

Besides the open G, you only need two chord shapes to play "Manu Kapalulu:"

Manu Kapalulu

"Sanoe," which you played in C tuning, only has these chords shapes:

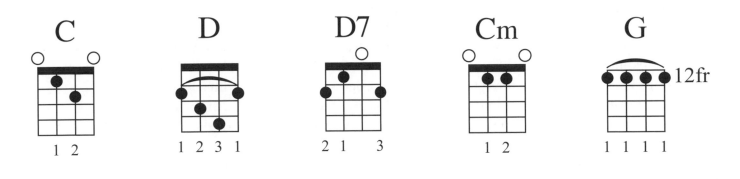

Sanoe

 35

"Wai O Ke Aniani," which means "crystal water," is a traditional Hawaiian love song whose lyrics, typically, combine nature and romance. Gabby Pahinui, who is regarded as the father of slack key guitar, recorded it in 1946. It was one of his earliest recorded vocal numbers.

Notice that both sections of this two-part tune end with a Hawaiian turnaround (marked in the music/tablature), sometimes called a "Hawaiian vamp." Songs of all descriptions (Hawaiian songs, American blues, pop, Tin Pan Alley, etc.) often feature a chord progression that ends with a V chord leading to a I chord. In traditional Hawaiian songs, including slack key tunes, this part of the progression is often repeated so that an "extra" two-bar turnaround (a bar of V and a bar of I) ends the progression. In a vocal number, the instrumental turnaround seems to echo the end of the vocal melody. In an instrumental, the turnaround is just an "extra" ending phrase. Many slack key players introduce a song with a turnaround, as well. In later Hawaiian music, the turnaround was expanded to a ii–V–I progression and was used to introduce songs as well as provide an extended ending to a chord progression.

Here are the chords that are used in this arrangement:

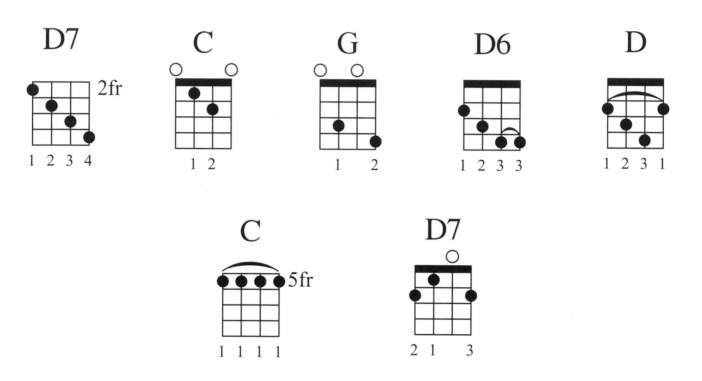

Wai O Ke Aniani

Unlike the C tuning version of "Ahe Lau Makani," this arrangement stays within the first five frets. It has two new chords:

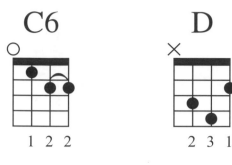

Ahe Lau Makani

"Kilakila 'O Haleakala" means "majestic Haleakala," referring to the dormant volcano crater on Maui. The first section of this tribute to the majestic mountain is usually performed at a lively tempo. Then it comes to a stop, and the second section (identical to the first except for the first few bars) is played at a slower tempo. You can end with part two (as in the arrangement below) or go back and repeat the faster first section, and then go around both parts as many times as you like.

It's hard to arrange this tune in open C or open G without losing some of the lowest notes or playing way up the neck. But the following arrangement in open G plays easily on the first five frets, because it's in the key of C. There's no law that says you have to play in G, just because you're tuned to an open G chord! This is rarely done in slack key—playing in a key other than the chord to which you're tuned—but it's seen occasionally.

This arrangement has one new chord shape:

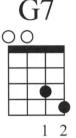

G7

Kilakila 'O Haleakala

Here's a G tuning arrangement of the beautiful, two-section "Ku'u Pua I Paoakalani."

It includes these new chords:

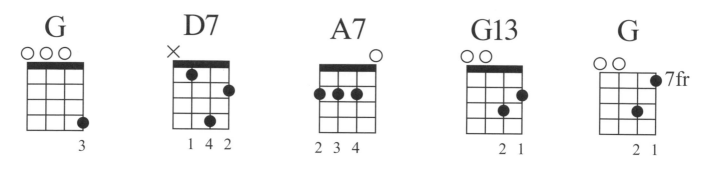

Ku'u Pua I Paoakalani

 39

G Tuning

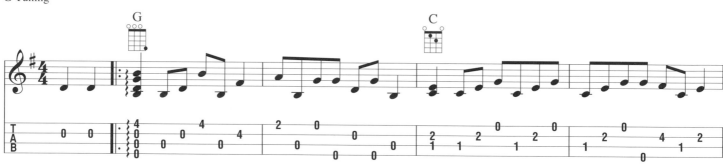

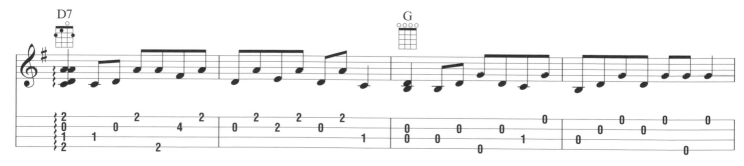

You played "Imi Au La Oe" in C tuning, harmonizing the melody (playing two strings at once). It's easier to play in G tuning! However, the second time around the 16-bar song, the harmonized melody is played up the neck an octave higher. This arrangement includes these very useful chord formations:

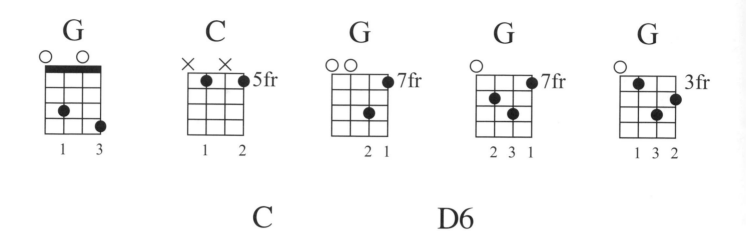

G   C   G   G   G

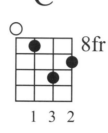

46

Imi Au La Oe

G Tuning

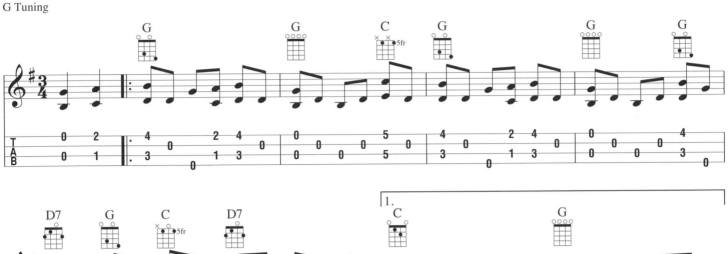

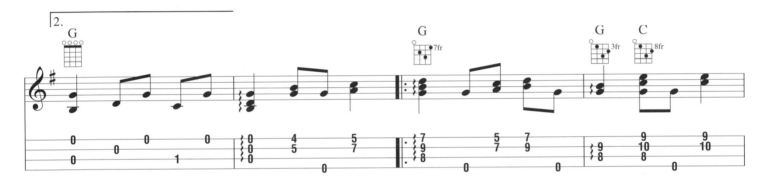

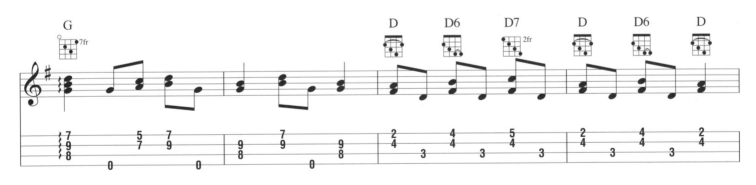

Slide in Standard Tuning

Standard ukulele tuning (G–C–E–A) is the same as open C tuning, except for the first string. With this in mind, you can play all your open C tuning songs and licks—if you compensate for that first A string being two frets higher.

For example, here's "Betty and Dupree" in standard tuning. It's almost exactly like the open C arrangement, but with adjustments made for the first string. Notice how the high fourth string G often substitutes for the first string when you adjust for the different tuning.

Betty and Dupree

41

The following solo for "Wreck of Old 97" is another example of how to adjust an open C tuning arrangement for standard tuning. Review the other version of the tune to compare it with this one.

Wreck of Old 97

Some tunes work well in the key of G in standard tuning. This version of "Beautiful Brown Eyes" shows how to get chords and melody with a slide without re-tuning your uke. This arrangement makes use of these chords:

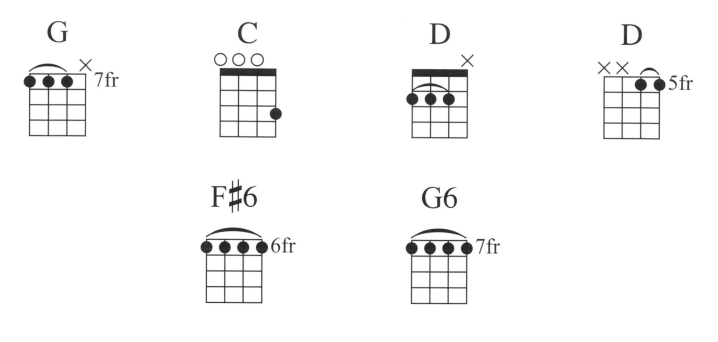

When barring chords like the G and D above, which exclude the first string, mute the open first string by touching it with the middle or ring finger of your picking hand.

Beautiful Brown Eyes

43

The following version of "Oh Mary, Don't You Weep" uses the same chords as "Wreck of Old 97," plus a few more:

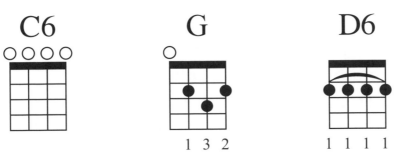

Oh Mary, Don't You Weep
Key of G

Many famous blues guitarists (both slide and non-slide players) favored the key of E. The long list includes Lightnin' Hopkins, Jimmy Reed, Gatemouth Brown, Guitar Slim, Arthur "Big Boy" Crudup, and Muddy Waters, who played all but his earliest slide recordings in standard tuning/E.

Quite a few of the iconic blues licks these players made famous can be duplicated on the ukulele in the key of A. Here's an 8-bar blues that shows how to play authentic blues slide licks in A, including a bluesy turnaround. The tune includes these chords (and partial, two-note chords):

8-Bar Blues
Key of A

You can also play non-blues slide tunes in A in standard tuning, such as this version of "Amazing Grace."

Amazing Grace
Key of A

Bessie Jones and the Georgia Sea Islanders may have been the first to record the gospel/folk tune, "Turkle Dove," also known as "Turtle Dove," but it has since been performed by folk and rock artists, including Jody Stecher and Jerry Garcia. This arrangement in the key of G consists of just two chords: G and D. There's plenty of back-and-forth between the first position G chord and the barred G chord at the seventh fret. Be careful not to play the first string when strumming the barred G and barred D chords.

Turkle Dove
Key of G

LISTENING SUGGESTIONS

One great way to pick up musical ideas is to listen to great players and try to imitate their licks, style, and overall feel. Here are some listening suggestions that include some of the most influential players; some have passed on, and some are still with us.

SLIDE PLAYERS

Ukulele players are just starting to play slide. But there are plenty of slide guitarists, Dobro players, and lap steel players worth listening to, including:

- **Blues/slide guitarists:** Elmore James, Blind Willie Johnson, Missippi Fred McDowell, Muddy Waters, Son House, Bukka White, Robert Johnson

- **Blues/rockers who often play slide:** Eric Clapton, Bonnie Raitt, Duane Allman, Ry Cooder, Derek Trucks, Warren Haynes

- **Dobro or acoustic lap-style players:** Josh Graves (with the Foggy Mountain Boys), Jerry Douglas, Rob Ickes, Sally Van Meter, Tut Taylor, Pete Kirby, Ben Harper, Kelly Joe Phelps

- **Lap steel heroes:** Jerry Byrd, David Lindley, Bob Dunn (with Milton Brown), Junior Brown, Cindy Cashdollar, Don Helms (with Hank Williams), Sol Hoʻopiʻi, Freddie Roulette, Sonny Rhodes

SLACK KEY GUITARISTS

Here are some of the greats, present and past: Gabby Pahinui, Sonny Chillingworth, Cyril Pahinui, Leonard Kwan, Atta Isaacs, Ray Kane, Dennis Kamakahi, Jeff Peterson, Makana, Patrick Landeza, Led Kaapana, and the Keola and Kapono Beamer (the Beamer Brothers).

Dancing Cat Records is an excellent source of slack key music.

ABOUT THE AUTHOR

Fred Sokolow is best known as the author of over 150 instructional and transcription books and DVDs for ukulele, guitar, banjo, Dobro, mandolin, and lap steel. Fred has long been a well-known West Coast multi-string performer and recording artist, particularly on the acoustic music scene. He has taught and performed at numerous ukulele camps and retreats. The diverse musical genres covered in his books and DVDs, along with several bluegrass, jazz, and rock CDs he has released, demonstrate his mastery of many musical styles. Whether he's playing Delta bottleneck blues, bluegrass/old-time banjo, 1930s swing guitar, or screaming rock solos, he does it with authenticity and passion.

Fred's other ukulele books include:

Fretboard Roadmaps for Ukulele, book/CD (with Jim Beloff), Hal Leonard Corporation

Blues Ukulele, book/CD, Flea Market Music, distributed by Hal Leonard Corporation

Bluegrass Ukulele, book/CD, Flea Market Music, distributed by Hal Leonard Corporation

101 Ukulele Tips, book/CD, Hal Leonard Corporation

Fingerstyle Ukulele, book/CD, Hal Leonard Corporation

Beatles Fingerstyle Ukulele, book/CD, Hal Leonard Corporation

Jazzing Up the Uke, book/CD, Flea Market Music, distributed by Hal Leonard Corporation

Email Fred with any questions about his guitar books at: Sokolowmusic.com.